'Tis the Season
QUILTS AND OTHER COMFORTS

Jeanne Large and Shelley Wicks

Martingale®
& COMPANY

Dedication

To our husbands, Tim and Jim, who keep the home fires burning
while we're off and running with our latest endeavor!

'Tis the Season: Quilts and Other Comforts
© 2010 by Jeanne Large and Shelley Wicks

That Patchwork Place

Martingale®
& COMPANY

That Patchwork Place® is an imprint of
Martingale & Company®.

Martingale & Company
20205 144th Avenue NE
Woodinville, WA 98072-8478
www.martingale-pub.com

Printed in China
15 14 13 12 11 10   8 7 6 5 4 3 2 1

**Library of Congress Cataloging-in-Publication Data
is available upon request.**

ISBN: 978-1-56477-984-7

Mission Statement

*Dedicated to providing quality products
and service to inspire creativity.*

Credits

President & CEO: Tom Wierzbicki
Editorial Director: Mary V. Green
Managing Editor: Tina Cook
Developmental Editor: Karen Costello Soltys
Technical Editor: Ursula Reikes
Copy Editor: Melissa Bryan
Design Director: Stan Green
Production Manager: Regina Girard
Illustrator: Laurel Strand
Cover & Text Designer: Adrienne Smitke
Photographer: Brent Kane

Contents

Introduction

'Tis the season . . . for family, friends, and traditions. As we prepare our homes for the holidays, it's fun to unpack treasures from past years and immerse ourselves in the memories those treasures evoke. Wouldn't it be great to unpack pillows, runners, and quilts, all with a holiday theme? Adding just a few accents to a room can change the feel of that space from everyday to holiday.

In the western Canadian province of Saskatchewan, we have cold and snow for at least five months of the year, sometimes longer. So, the weather alone inspires us to make quilts and use them as part of our decor. It's nice on those chilly winter evenings to cuddle under a quilt while reading or watching TV. We believe in using our quilts, so every quilt we make is washable. Besides, a quilt is simply more inviting after it's been laundered. A quilt that appears crinkly and soft looks more approachable and is more likely to be pulled out and used.

Quilts can be so much more than a blanket on a bed. We hope this book will inspire you to use your quilts throughout your home in your holiday decorating. The projects are simple as well as charming. They're destined to give your holiday decorating spirit a boost.

Try using a quilt instead of a traditional tree skirt. Choose a quilt in colors that work with your holiday theme. If your quilt tops don't work, check out the backings—one of them might be just the right color. Spread the quilt under the tree, and then scrunch it up to shape it around the tree stand.

Fabric Selection and Preparation

Fabric is what quiltmaking is all about, so choosing and preparing it wisely is always a good investment of time. Every project, no matter how large or small, begins with choosing fabric colors and designs. This can be the most enjoyable aspect of a new project for some, or the most dreaded.

We love the "choosing fabrics" part of a new quilt, and often we choose more than one colorway before coming to a decision. Fabric selection can involve a lot of discussion and a huge mess! It's helpful to see all the fabrics for a project together on a table. Being able to view them in a single grouping gives you a feel for the overall appeal of the finished project. You'll be able to see if you have a balance of light and dark and if the color you want to highlight really does show well. Most important, when you look at the group of fabrics you've chosen, do you like it? Is there one piece that draws your eye and distracts from the others? You may be happier without that piece.

It's a good idea to vary the scale of your prints. A plaid, striped, or polka-dot fabric can add texture to your project but still blend well with floral prints. Again, stand back and view the fabrics together. Is the overall effect pleasing? Trust yourself—it's *your* quilt!

We tend to choose earth tones and pair them with strong contrasting colors. Using one consistent color can ground a quilt, while accommodating the use of lots of other colors for a scrappy look. You'll see this with the use of the black fabrics in both in "Vintage Cherries" and "Winter Cottage Wall Quilt." In the quilts "Snowballs" and "The Stockings Were Hung," we used a single background fabric. A solid black background offers the opportunity to add any color, while a colored print narrows your choices to fabrics that work with that print.

In our holiday quilts, we like to use a good variety of fabrics rather than holiday-specific prints. Check your local quilt shop for fabrics that will work with your decorating theme.

To Prewash or Not to Prewash

Prewashing is such a controversial topic. There's no right or wrong answer; you must decide what's best for you. We choose not to prewash any of our quilting fabrics.

If you're purchasing good, quality fabrics from a quilt shop, you should be fine without prewashing. The fabric-printing process has improved immensely over the years, and very few quality fabrics will give you a problem.

If you're concerned about the color quality of a fabric, it's a good idea to test a piece before using it in a quilt. Place a small piece of the fabric in a hot water bath with a touch of detergent. Swish the fabric around a bit, and then place it on a white paper towel. Blot with paper towels and let the fabric dry. If any color has transferred onto the paper towels, you might want to consider using a different fabric. Certainly you could wash this fabric over and over again to try to remove the excess dye, but it will still present a high risk. It's a better idea to choose a different fabric.

We're partial to the crisp feel of fabric before the sizing has been washed out, but if you choose to prewash, there are some fabulous spray starches on the market, specifically for quilters, and they will put that crispness back in your fabric.

Although the shrinkage rate of good-quality 100% cotton is minimal these days, it's best to use cold water when washing a completed quilt and a warm—not hot—setting on your dryer. You should end up with a quilt that has a slightly crinkled look, with a soft and snuggly feel to it.

Using Fat Quarters

A fat quarter is a half yard of fabric cut in half along the fold line, which yields a piece of fabric approximately 18" x 21".

When a pattern calls for a width of fabric, this means the width from selvage to selvage. So a fat quarter will be about 21" wide. When cutting a fat quarter, lay the selvage edge parallel to the bottom edge of your cutting mat.

Our Favorite Special Techniques

In this section you'll find all our favorite appliqué techniques, plus some of the special techniques we used in our projects.

Appliqué

We love adding appliqué to our quilts and think that simple appliqué can elevate even the most basic block to something stunning. There are many appliqué methods, and we encourage you to use what works well for you. However, because we believe that Christmas projects shouldn't take a huge amount of your time during the holiday season, we prefer techniques that can be executed quickly. Here we'll share two of our preferred methods.

Fusible web works well for small appliqué shapes. It's an easy trace, cut, and paste method that's quick to do and fuses the shapes onto the background fabric, ready to be stitched down by hand or by machine.

For large, chunky shapes, we like to use fusible interfacing. This method gives you a clean, turned-under edge with the shape fused down, ready to be stitched on by hand or machine.

FUSIBLE-WEB APPLIQUÉ

Before you begin a project using fusible web, we encourage you to read the directions that come with it for guidelines on heat settings and fusing times. We recommend using a lightweight product. Anything too heavy tends to gum up the needle, is harder to sew through, and will add a stiff feeling to your quilts.

When using fusible-web appliqué, you need to be sure the shapes are reversed from the image shown in the completed quilt. The images in this book have already been reversed for you.

1. Using a pencil, trace the appliqué shapes onto the paper side of the fusible product, leaving at least 1" between each shape.

2. Cut the appliqué shapes out of the fusible web, *outside* of the pencil line. If you like, you could also cut out the fusible web from the middle of each piece, leaving ¼" to ½" *inside* the pencil line. Cutting away the interior of a shape helps keep your appliqué pieces soft to the touch when the stitching is finished.

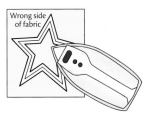

3. Following the manufacturer's instructions for the fusible product, adhere each shape, traced side up, onto the *wrong* side of the desired fabric. Press; don't iron. You don't want your shapes moving around.

Wrong side of fabric

- - ♪rom The Quilt Patch - - - - - - - -

There is a big difference between pressing and ironing.

Pressing means gently lowering your iron onto the fabric, holding the iron for a few seconds, and then lifting it and bringing it down gently at another spot on the fabric. Pressing is preferred for fusible products so that they don't accidentally move under the iron and become fused in a place you don't want them to be.

Ironing means bringing the iron down and gliding it back and forth. Ironing is great for removing wrinkles from clothing or large pieces of fabric.

~ Shelley

4. Allow all fabrics to cool. Carefully cut out each appliqué piece directly on the drawn line. Remove the paper backing from each piece.

5. Using your ironing board as a work surface, arrange the shapes on the background fabric or blocks, referring to the pattern for proper placement. Be sure all shapes are tucked under or overlapped where they should be. Press the appliqués in place.

6. Sew the raw edges of all the appliqué shapes to the background fabric either by hand or machine. The stitch we most commonly use is a blanket stitch. The thread you choose can coordinate with the fabric, or you may prefer a contrasting thread for a more primitive look.

┌ - *From The Quilt Patch* - - - - - - - ┐

When blanket stitching by machine, use an open-toe presser foot. It enables you to better see where you're going and how your stitches are forming.

~ Jeanne

└ - - - - - - - - - - - - - - - - - - - ┘

FUSIBLE-INTERFACING APPLIQUÉ

Before you start a project using fusible interfacing, you may want to test various brands on the market—one company's version of a lightweight product may be like another's medium-weight interfacing. Try a few and find the one that works best for you. We recommend a lightweight interfacing; whether to choose a woven or nonwoven product depends on your preference. The fusible interfacing remains in the appliqué, so it's important to use one that is easy to work with but won't make your appliqué overly stiff.

1. Using a pencil, trace the appliqué shapes onto the nonfusible side of the fusible interfacing, reversing the shapes if necessary and leaving at least 2" between each shape.

2. Cut the appliqué shapes out of the fusible interfacing, *outside* of the pencil line, leaving at least 1" seam allowance.

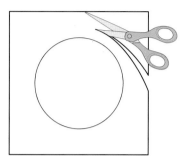

3. Lay a fusible interfacing shape with the fusible side against the *right* side of the chosen fabric. Pin in place. Sew directly on the drawn line, all around the entire shape.

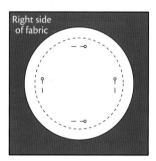

Right side of fabric

4. Trim around the shape, leaving approximately ⅛" for seam allowance all around. Carefully make a slit in the center of the fusible interfacing, enough to be able to turn the shape right side out.

5. Once the shape is turned, gently run your finger or a blunt object around the inside of the shape along the seam line to help ease the edges out. The fusible side of the product is now facing out, and the raw edges are on the inside.

Arrange your shape on the background fabric or block, referring to the pattern for proper placement. Gently press the appliqué in place with a hot iron.

6. If your sewing machine has a blind hem stitch in its functions, you can program that stitch so the point of the V just nips into the appliqué. Using an invisible thread will give the look of hand appliqué. Another option would be a zig-zag stitch, or you can blanket stitch by hand.

Working with Wool

Incorporating wool into a project adds an unexpected texture, a richness of color, and a great primitive look.

PREPARING THE WOOL

We like to use 100% wool that's been felted. Felting your own wool is no more difficult than washing a load of clothes. Throw your wool into a hot-wash, cold-rinse setting. Wool is made of interlocking fibers, and this extreme temperature change causes the fibers to interlock more tightly. Dry the wool in a hot dryer. Throwing a towel into the dryer with the wool adds to the agitation and gives you a more supple product. Yes, the wool will shrink, but once it's felted you can use it in a quilt and it won't continue to shrink with future washings.

Wool that's been felted doesn't usually have a right or wrong side—they both look the same. In addition, felted wool usually doesn't fray. If you find your wool is still fraying, you could wash and dry it again and again until you're satisfied with the density of the finished product.

Woolen yard goods that are loosely woven are not likely to felt nicely. Learning which wools felt nicely and which ones don't is sometimes just a matter of trial and error. Nice wool is pricey, so the old adage "you get what you pay for" definitely rings true here. If you come across some bargain wool, it may not be worth even a bargain price.

APPLIQUÉING WITH WOOL

Fusible-web method. We usually use fusible web for our wool appliqués. Be sure to carefully read the instructions with the product you're using. An iron that's too hot can scorch the wool.

If you find it difficult to fuse the wool appliqué shape to the cotton background fabric, try pinning in place, flipping the project over, and pressing well from the back. The heat will easily penetrate the cotton background, melting the glue and fusing your wool shape down.

If you're layering wool appliqué shapes, we have found it works best to fuse one layer at a time.

Freezer-paper method. If you plan to stitch your wool appliqué shapes to your project by hand, you can skip the fusible web and use freezer paper to make accurate cutting templates.

Trace the appliqué shapes onto the unwaxed side of the freezer paper. Cut loosely around the shape, leaving about ½" of paper outside of your pencil line. Lay the shiny side of the freezer paper on the wool and gently press down with a dry iron on a medium setting.

The wax on the freezer paper will melt enough to stick the paper to the wool. Cut out the shape directly on your drawn line. Peel the freezer paper off and your wool shape is ready to hand stitch to your project.

Special Techniques

We like to use hand embroidery and a few other types of decorative embellishments on our projects. They're fun and easy to do while adding lots of visual punch.

HAND-EMBROIDERY STITCHES

A fine pearl cotton or two strands of embroidery floss works well for these simple hand stitches. Be sure to use an embroidery needle with a large eye. The stitching is always done before the quilt top is layered, basted, and quilted, so the back of your work is hidden.

Backstitch

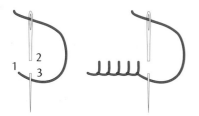

Blanket stitch

Running stitch

MAKING VINES

We often use a vine as part of our appliqué design. Adding a new texture to a project can be fun, and vines offer a perfect opportunity to use rickrack or wool even if the rest of the project is cotton.

The revival of rickrack. Yes, it's back! And it makes a wonderful vine, flower stem, or accent on a quilt. Rickrack comes in many colors and a variety of widths, so you have lots of options. You also have several choices when sewing it to your

project. If your project is something that you'll never wash, just pin your vine in place and sew down the center of the strip by machine. However, if you're using rickrack on a quilt that you're likely going to launder, it's a good idea to sew it down on both outside edges so you won't have to worry that they will roll up or distort in any way when your quilt is washed. You can sew the edges using a machine blanket stitch or a straight stitch, or you can stitch them by hand.

Using wool strips. Strips of wool make fabulous vines or flower stems. Even if there's no other wool in your project, wool vines will add some interest and texture to your appliqué. Before using wool it should be felted; see page 9 for instructions on wool preparation. We use strips of wool cut $\frac{3}{8}$" wide. Wool usually doesn't need to be cut on the bias, since the nature of wool makes it easy to shape and manipulate as long as the strips are not too wide. Lay the vine on the background fabric as desired and pin in place. Sew the edges in place using a blanket stitch, by hand or machine.

Bias vines from cotton. Cotton vines are easy to make and cutting them on the bias makes them easy to shape. We suggest starting with an 18" to 20" square of fabric.

1. Lay your fabric on the cutting mat and cut the square in half diagonally. If you have a 45° line on your cutting mat you can use it as a guideline. Using the diagonal line you have just cut as your guide, continue to cut diagonal strips of fabric. Usually a 1½" strip will give you a bias vine that's wide enough for good visual impact but narrow enough to manipulate easily.

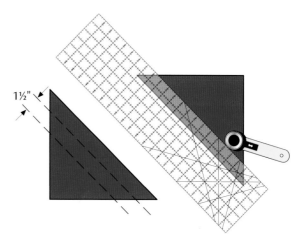

2. Sew the strips together to achieve the length required. With right sides together, join the strips at right angles as shown. Press the seam allowances open.

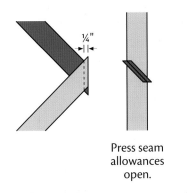

Press seam
allowances
open.

3. Lay the strip right side down on your ironing board. Fold in half lengthwise and press with wrong sides together.

4. Fold the raw edges toward the folded edge of the long strip. Keep the raw edges slightly behind, not even with, the folded edge. Press. The raw edges will be hidden beneath the vine, but you'll also have some flexibility in the width you choose to create your vine. Now you have a folded edge on both sides of your vine.

5. Shape and pin the vine in place as shown in your project instructions. Secure in place with a hand or machine blanket stitch.

From The Quilt Patch

When using a machine blanket stitch to secure the vine, we find it helpful to use a walking foot to alleviate the stretch that inevitably occurs when with working with bias fabric. Your vine will lie nice and flat with no visible bumps or ripples.

Basting by hand would be an alternative if you don't have a walking foot for your machine.

~ Jeanne

Finishing Basics

Good finishing techniques are essential to the completed quilt. While we don't have room to cover all of the finishing options, we'll share a few of our favorite ideas.

BORDERS

When your quilt top is complete and it's time to add the borders, we recommend you measure your quilt top to ensure that it matches up with the size of borders the project instructions tell you to cut. Sometimes the difference in seam allowances can create a bit of discrepancy in the finished size of the quilt top. Carefully checking your measurements and adjusting the border lengths accordingly will ensure that your quilt lies flat and will avoid borders that are too tight or fall in waves.

Be sure your quilt top is well pressed. Lay it out flat and measure vertically through the center and the sides (not directly on the edge of your quilt, but in about 6"). If the measurements differ from each other, take the average of the three measurements and cut the two vertical borders to that length.

Fold these border strips in half crosswise to find the center. Do the same with the quilt top. Pin the center of the border to the center of the side of the quilt top. Align the ends of the quilt top and the ends of the border, and pin in place. Add more pins between these pinpoints, easing any fullness or gently stretching as required.

Sew the borders to the sides of the quilt top. Press. Repeat this process for the top and bottom borders, taking measurements horizontally.

Need a larger area for pressing borders and appliqué? Make your own ironing board! Cut a piece of ½" plywood to measure approximately 5" larger all around than your existing ironing board. Leave the board in a rectangular shape. Cut two pieces of cotton batting to measure 3" larger all around than your board. Cut a piece of muslin slightly larger than the batting.

Lay the muslin on the floor. Lay the two layers of batting on top, centered, with some muslin showing on all sides. Center the board on top. Pull the muslin over the edge of the wood and staple the fabric to the wood along one side using a staple gun. On the opposite side, pull the muslin as taut as possible over the edge of the wood and staple in place. Repeat for each end of your board. Trim the batting diagonally across each corner. Fold the muslin over the corners and staple in place.

Now you have a large pressing surface to use on a table or countertop. If you choose to use this on top of your ironing board, be careful to center the ironing board underneath and keep your iron on a separate, more stable surface when not in use.

BACKING

Backing fabric offers a great opportunity to use a large-scale floral or a bold print that looks good with your quilt but just doesn't work into the top of your quilt. Plush fabrics are available in a 60" width and make a great backing for a lap quilt. Most plush fabrics are 100% polyester and commonly referred to as "minkee." There are many different brands and qualities on the market, so it's important to be selective. Your choice of backing fabric is important; be sure it coordinates with your quilt top and is of good quality.

The batting and backing should always be cut larger than your quilt top—usually about 3" to 4" larger on all sides. If you're hiring a professional long-arm quilter to do your quilting, check with the quilter first for his or her specifications regarding backing and batting sizes before you cut these pieces.

BATTING

We use an 80/20 blend—80% cotton, 20% polyester. We find this thin batting gives a nice drape and is great for both hand and machine quilting. Plus, after washing the quilt, this batting gives that nice, crinkly antique look we love.

BINDING

All our projects use double-fold binding cut in 2½"-wide strips. The yardages listed in this book allow for enough binding to go around the perimeter of the quilt, plus extra for joining the strips and mitering the corners.

1. Cut the binding fabric across its width, unless otherwise specified, into the number of 2½" strips required.
2. With right sides together, join the binding strips at right angles as shown to make one long strip. Trim excess seam allowance and press the seams open to reduce bulk.

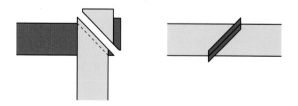

3. Cut one end at a 45° angle, turn that end under ¼", and press in place. Fold the strip in half lengthwise, with wrong sides together, and press.

Fold line

4. Lay the raw edges of the binding even with the edge of the quilt top. Place the end midway down one edge and start sewing approximately 10" from the start of the binding strip. Sew through all the layers using a ¼" seam allowance, stopping ¼" from the first corner. Backstitch, clip the threads, and remove the quilt from the machine.

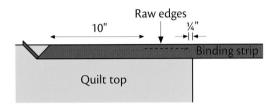

5. Turn the quilt so you're ready to sew the next side. Fold the binding straight back, away from the quilt, and then back down on itself so that the raw edge is even with the quilt edge again. Stitch from the fold, backstitching at the edge of the quilt. This fold will create a mitered corner when you turn the binding to the back of the quilt and blindstitch it in place. Continue sewing the binding to the edges of the quilt, repeating the mitering process at the remaining corners.

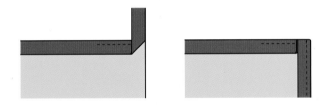

6. When you're approximately 10" to 12" from where you started, stop sewing and backstitch. Cut the remaining tail of binding at an angle 1" longer than needed. Tuck the tail into the starting diagonal edge. Finish sewing the binding.

7. Bring the folded edge of the binding over to the back of the quilt, covering the raw edges of the quilt. Be sure the binding covers the sewing line. Use a thread that matches the binding and blindstitch in place, mitering the corners as you come to them.

Inspiring Ideas

Keep an eye out at secondhand stores and flea markets for old ladders. We have one that came from Jeanne's grandparents' farm. After a good scrubbing with a wire brush and soapy water, it makes a wonderful stand for displaying quilts. Leaned against a wall and draped with just one quilt or layered with several quilts, a ladder makes a great prop in practically any room in your home.

High Strung

The scrappy border gives this quilt a fun, eclectic look that appeals to all ages.
Whether you use this quilt as a wall hanging or drape it over the back of a sofa
to cozy up with on cool evenings, it will bring a smile to your heart!

FINISHED QUILT: 46½" x 62½"

Designed and pieced by Jeanne Large and Shelley Wicks.
Machine quilted by Laila Nelson.

Materials

Yardages are based on 42"-wide fabric unless otherwise specified.

11 fat quarters in various shades of green for blocks and outer border

1⅓ yards of beige fabric for appliqué background

½ yard of red fabric for inner border

1 fat quarter of red fabric for stockings

10" x 10" piece of coordinating red fabric for heels and toes

2 fat quarters of green fabric for trees and holly leaves

1 fat quarter of green fabric or a 1" x 45" strip of green felted wool for vine

8" x 12" piece of gold fabric for stars

8" x 14" piece of brown fabric for tree trunks

½ yard of red fabric for binding

3¼ yards of fabric for backing

56" x 72" piece of batting

2 yards of lightweight fusible web for appliqués

Thread for blanket-stitching around appliqué shapes

21 red buttons in various diameters from ¼" to 1" for holly berries

Cutting

Cut all strips across the width of fabric unless otherwise specified.

From the *lengthwise grain* of the beige fabric, cut:

1 rectangle, 16½" x 40½"

From *each* of the 11 fat quarters of green for blocks and outer border, cut:

1 strip, 2½" x 20" (11 total)

2 strips, 5½" x 20" (22 total); crosscut each strip into 3 squares, 5½" x 5½" (66 total; 2 will be extra)

From the red inner-border fabric, cut:

6 strips, 1½" x 42"

From the red binding fabric, cut:

6 strips, 2½" x 42"

Appliqué

1. Referring to "Fusible-Web Appliqué" on page 7 and using the patterns on pages 18 and 19, prepare the following:
   - 3 stockings from red fabric
   - 2 stockings *reversed* from red fabric
   - 3 heels and 3 toes from coordinating red fabric
   - 2 heels and 2 toes *reversed* from coordinating red fabric
   - 2 trees from green fabric
   - 2 trees *reversed* from green fabric
   - 22 holly leaves from green fabric
   - 2 tree trunks from brown fabric
   - 2 tree trunks *reversed* from brown fabric
   - 6 stars from gold fabric

2. Refer to "Making Vines" on page 10 to prepare the vine. You'll need approximately 45" of vine.

3. Using the photo as a guide, arrange the shapes on the beige 16½" x 40½" panel and fuse in place. Appliqué them by hand or machine.

Assembling the Quilt Top

1. Arrange the green 5½" squares into eight rows of eight squares each.

2. Sew the squares together into rows. Press the seam allowances in opposite directions from row to row. Sew seven of the eight rows of blocks together. Press the seam allowances in the same direction.

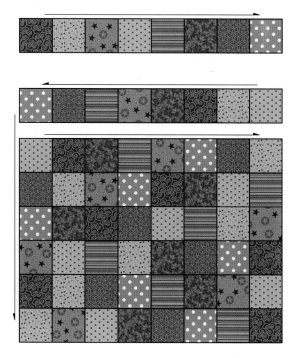

3. Sew the appliqué panel to the top row of blocks, and then join the remaining row of blocks to the top edge of the appliqué panel. Press.

Adding the Borders

1. Sew the red 1½" x 42" inner-border strips together end to end to make one continuous strip. Cut two strips, 56½" long, and two strips, 42½" long. Sew the 56½"-long strips to the sides of the quilt. Press. Sew the 42½"-long strips to the top and bottom of the quilt. Press.

2. Sew the green 2½" x 20" outer-border strips together end to end to make one continuous strip. Cut two strips, 58½" long, and two strips, 46½" long. Sew the 58½"-long strips to the sides of the quilt. Press. Sew the 46½"-long strips to the top and bottom of the quilt. Press.

Finishing the Quilt

Refer to "Finishing Basics" on page 11 for detailed instructions as needed.

1. Layer the backing, batting, and quilt top. Baste.
2. Quilt as desired. Our quilt was machine quilted with an allover design of stars and loops.
3. After quilting, randomly sew the red buttons onto the vine for holly berries.
4. Bind the quilt using the red 2½"-wide strips.

Inspiring Ideas

If you have an unheated front porch that could benefit from some holiday ambiance, toss a quilt over a comfy couch, add a bowl of sparkly vintage Christmas balls and a few sprigs of Christmas greenery, and you've turned a forlorn, unused space into a warm and inviting vignette.

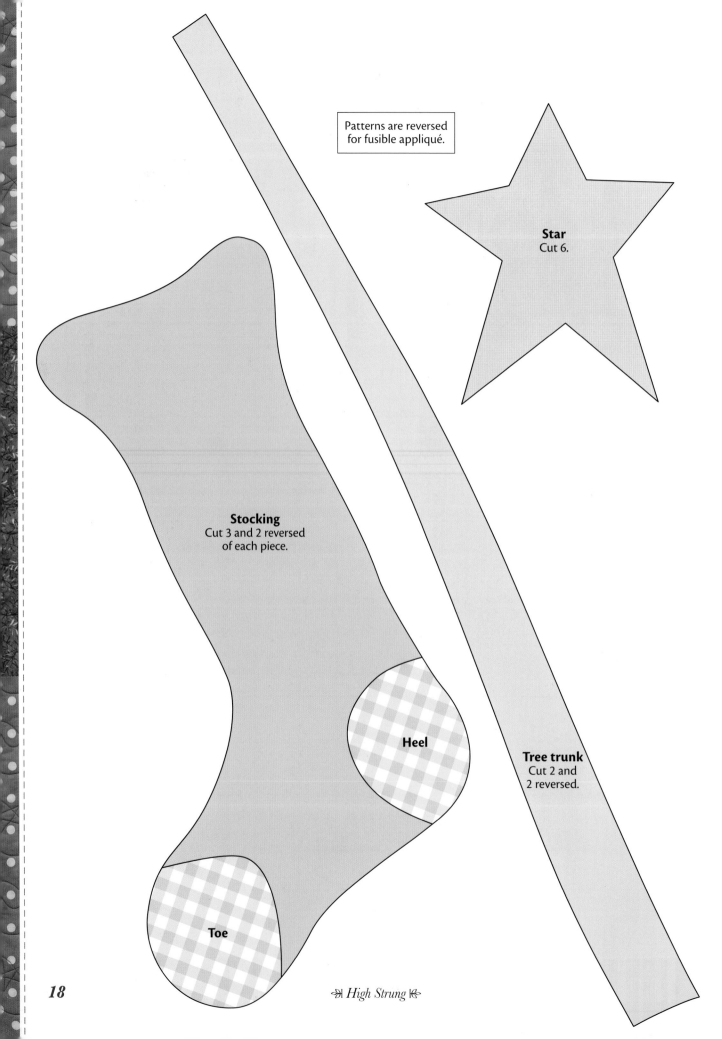

Patterns are reversed for fusible appliqué.

Star
Cut 6.

Stocking
Cut 3 and 2 reversed of each piece.

Heel

Tree trunk
Cut 2 and 2 reversed.

Toe

High Strung

Patterns are reversed for fusible appliqué.

Tree
Cut 2 and 2 reversed.

Holly leaf
Cut 22.

Joy to the World Pillow

Add some joy to your world with this holiday pillow. It's perfect for dressing up a guest room, where you can use it as a bolster for a fun and welcome addition to the bedding.

FINISHED PILLOW: 15½" x 41½"

Materials

Yardages are based on 42"-wide fabric unless otherwise specified.

1⅓ yards of black flannel for pillow front and back

20" x 20" piece of red fabric for letters

6" x 18" piece of green fabric for leaves

1 fat quarter of green fabric or a 1" x 45" strip of green felted wool for vine

6" x 11" piece of gold fabric for stars

12 red buttons in various diameters from ¼" to 1" for holly berries

1 yard of lightweight fusible web for appliqués

Thread for blanket-stitching around appliqué shapes

18" x 44" piece of batting

18" x 44" piece of muslin

Fiberfill stuffing

Cutting

From the *lengthwise grain* of the black flannel, cut:

2 rectangles, 16" x 42"

Assembling the Pillow

1. Referring to "Fusible-Web Appliqué" on page 7 and using the patterns on pages 22 and 23, prepare the following:
   - Letters to spell "Joy to the World" from red fabric
   - 8 holly leaves from green fabric
   - 6 stars from gold fabric

2. Refer to "Making Vines" on page 10 to prepare the vine. You'll need approximately 44" of vine.

3. Using the photo as a guide, arrange the shapes on the pillow front and fuse in place. Appliqué them by hand or machine.

4. With the right side up, lay the pillow front on top of the 18" x 44" piece of batting, and then on the piece of muslin. Baste the layers. Quilt the pillow top as desired. Our pillow has large stippling in the background around the shapes.

From The Quilt Patch

A good pair of quilting gloves—cotton gloves with gripper dots on the palms and fingertips—is a must for machine quilting. They take the stress off of your neck and shoulders by making it easier to grip the fabric. Whether your project is large or small, pull them out and slip them on.

~ Shelley

Designed and made by Jeanne Large.

5. Trim the batting to the same size as the pillow front.

6. Sew the 12 red buttons onto the vine in clusters of three for holly berries.

7. Lay the pillow front and pillow back with right sides together and raw edges even. Sew around the outside edge of the pillow, leaving a 6" opening along one edge.

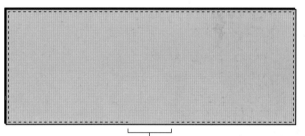

Leave a 6" opening for turning.

8. Turn the pillow right side out. Stuff firmly and hand stitch the opening closed.

Inspiring Ideas

Try using this pillow on top of a cupboard in a nest of greenery. Add miniature lights or garland for extra color and sparkle.

Patterns are reversed
for fusible appliqué.

Patterns are reversed
for fusible appliqué.

Star
Cut 6.

Holly leaf
Cut 8.

Winter Cottage Trio

Make the matching pillow and runner to go with this lap quilt and you have the perfect winter set that will work in your decor before and beyond the holiday season.

Winter Cottage Lap Quilt

FINISHED QUILT: 48½" x 56½"
FINISHED BLOCK: 8" x 8"

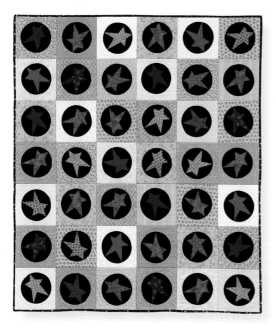

Designed and made by Jeanne Large and Shelley Wicks.

Materials

Yardages are based on 42"-wide fabric.

⅓ yard *each* of 11 different medium to dark beige fabrics for backgrounds
2 yards of black flannel for circles
⅛ yard *each* of 9 assorted fabrics for stars
½ yard of black fabric for binding
3¼ yards of fabric for backing
58" x 66" piece of batting
2 yards of lightweight fusible interacting for circles
2 yards of lightweight fusible web for stars
Thread for blanket-stitching around appliqué shapes

The materials list contains sufficient fabric to make the quilt. The actual quilt is more scrappy than what's called for. If you enjoy a more scrappy look, feel free to add more fabrics.

Cutting

Cut all strips across the width of fabric.

From *each* of the 11 beige background fabrics, cut:
1 strip, 8½" x 42"; crosscut each strip into 4 squares, 8½" x 8½" (44 total; 2 will be extra)

From the black flannel, cut:
9 strips, 7" x 42"; crosscut each strip into 5 squares, 7" x 7" (45 total; 3 will be extra)

From the black binding fabric, cut:
6 strips, 2½" x 42"

Appliqué

1. Referring to "Fusible-Interfacing Appliqué" on page 8 and using the circle pattern on page 27, prepare 42 black flannel circles.
2. Place each circle on an 8½" background square. Press in place and appliqué by hand or machine.

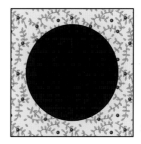

Make 42.

3. Referring to "Fusible-Web Appliqué" on page 7 and using the star pattern on page 27, prepare 42 shapes from the nine different star fabrics. Fuse the stars in place and appliqué them by hand or machine.

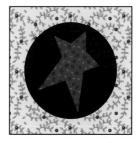

Make 42.

Assembling the Quilt Top

1. Arrange the blocks randomly into seven rows of six blocks each.
2. Sew the blocks together into rows. Press the seam allowances in opposite directions from row to row. Sew the rows together. Press the seam allowances in the same direction.

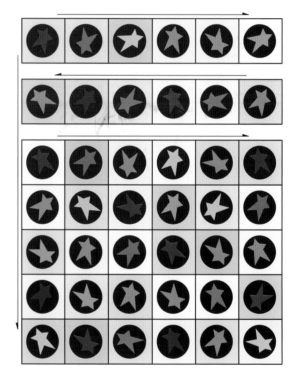

Finishing the Quilt

Refer to "Finishing Basics" on page 11 for detailed instructions as needed.

1. Layer the backing, batting, and quilt top. Baste.
2. Quilt as desired. Our quilt has simple stitch-in-the-ditch machine quilting.
3. Bind the quilt using the black 2½"-wide strips.

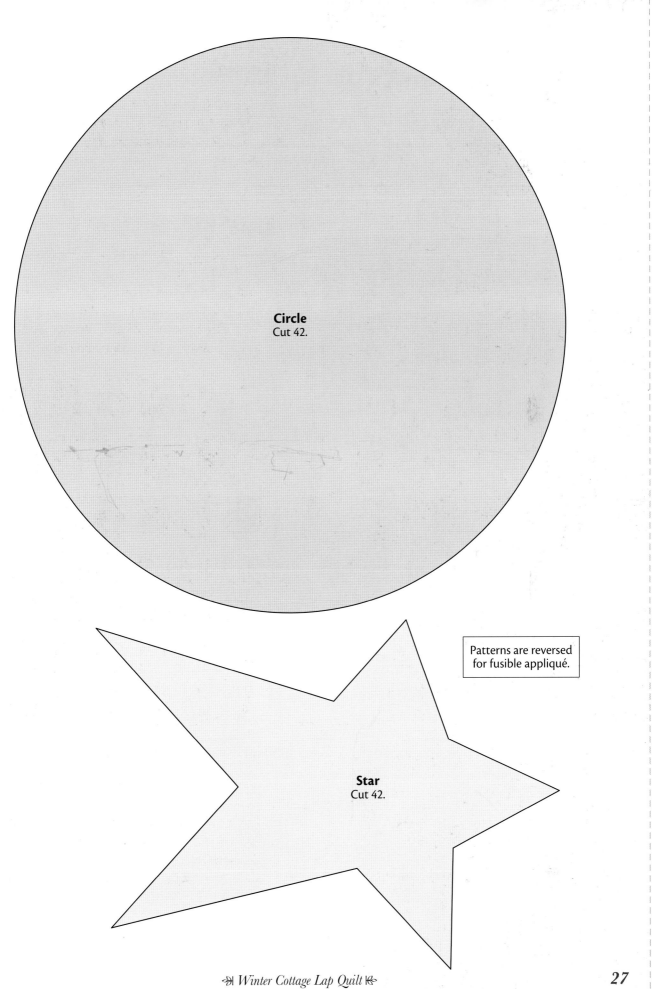

Circle
Cut 42.

Patterns are reversed
for fusible appliqué.

Star
Cut 42.

Winter Cottage Runner

FINISHED SIZE: 12½" x 20½"
FINISHED BLOCK: 4" x 4"

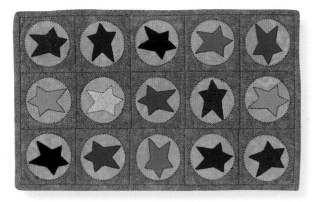

Designed and made by Jeanne Large.

Materials

Yardages are based on 42"-wide fabric.

½ yard of gray flannel for background and binding
¼ yard of gold fabric for circles
4 pieces of felted wool, 6" x 8", in various colors
    for stars
½ yard of fabric for backing
14" x 23" piece of batting
1 yard of lightweight fusible web for appliqués
Thread for blanket-stitching around appliqué shapes

The materials list contains sufficient fabric to make the runner. The actual runner is more scrappy than what's called for. If you enjoy a more scrappy look, feel free to add more fabrics.

Cutting

Cut all strips across the width of fabric.

From the gray flannel, cut:
2 strips, 4½" x 42"; crosscut a total of 15 squares,
    4½" x 4½"
2 strips, 2½" x 42"

Appliqué

1. Referring to "Fusible-Web Appliqué" on page 7 and using the circle pattern on the facing page, prepare 15 circles from gold fabric.
2. Place each circle on a 4½" background square. Fuse in place and appliqué the shapes by hand or machine.
3. Referring to "Appliquéing with Wool" on page 9 and using the star pattern on the facing page, prepare a total of 15 stars from the four pieces of felted wool.
4. Place one star on each circle and appliqué the shapes by hand or machine.

Make 15.

Make 15.

Assembling the Runner

1. Arrange the blocks into three rows of five blocks each.
2. Sew the squares together into rows. Press the seam allowances in opposite directions from row to row. Sew the rows together. Press the seam allowances in one direction.

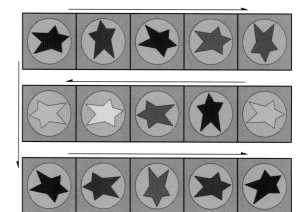

Finishing the Runner

Refer to "Finishing Basics" on page 11 for detailed instructions as needed

1. Layer the backing, batting, and runner top. Baste the layers.
2. Quilt as desired. Our runner is finished with simple stitch-in-the-ditch machine quilting.
3. Bind the runner using the gray 2½"-wide flannel strips.

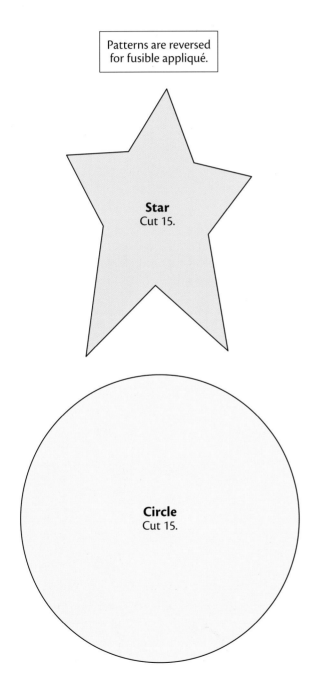

Patterns are reversed for fusible appliqué.

Star
Cut 15.

Circle
Cut 15.

Winter Cottage Pillow

FINISHED SIZE: 10" x 18"

Designed and made by Jeanne Large.

Materials

Yardages are based on 42"-wide fabric.

⅓ yard of black flannel for pillow front and back
3 pieces of felted wool, 6½" x 6½", in various colors for circles
3 pieces of felted wool, 4½" x 6", in various colors for stars
Thread for blanket-stitching around appliqué shapes
12" x 20" piece of batting
12" x 20" piece of muslin
Fiberfill stuffing

Cutting

From the black flannel, cut:
2 pieces, 10½" x 18½"

Giving a room a theme makes it easy to add accessories. Stars are a striking yet simple decorating motif. Add some dishes with a starry pattern, hang some wooden or metal stars, or light some star-shaped candles. Using several star-related projects in one room can give the space a primitive, country feeling in an instant.

Appliqué

1. Referring to "Appliquéing with Wool" on page 9 and using the patterns on the facing page, prepare the following:
   - 3 circles from the 6½" x 6½" pieces of felted wool
   - 3 stars from the 4½" x 6" pieces of felted wool

2. Using the photo on page 29 as a guide, arrange the circles and stars on the pillow front. Appliqué them by hand or machine.

Finishing

1. With right side facing up, lay the pillow front on top of the 12" x 20" piece of batting, and then on top of the piece of muslin. Baste the layers. Quilt the pillow front. One option would be to stitch around each appliqué shape to outline it. Since this is a small project, it would also be fine to leave it unquilted.

2. Trim the batting to the same size as the pillow front.

3. Lay the pillow front and pillow back with right sides together and raw edges even. Sew around the outside edge of the pillow, leaving a 6" opening along one edge.

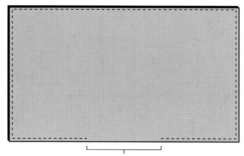

Leave a 6" opening for turning.

4. Turn the pillow right side out. Stuff firmly with fiberfill and hand stitch the opening closed.

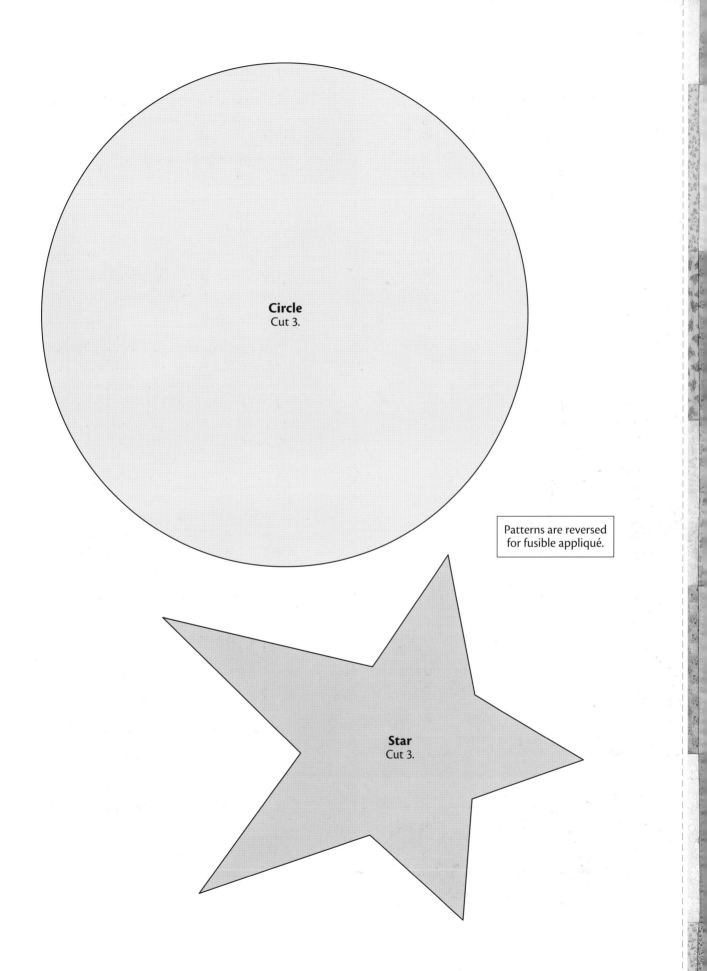

Circle
Cut 3.

Patterns are reversed
for fusible appliqué.

Star
Cut 3.

Vintage Cherries

Pull your favorite fat quarters from your stash to make this fabulous quilt.
It will be a winner well beyond the holiday season.

FINISHED QUILT: 60½" x 72½"
FINISHED BLOCK: 6" x 6"

Designed and made by Jeanne Large and Shelley Wicks.
Machine quilted by Laila Nelson.

Materials

Yardages are based on 42"-wide fabric unless otherwise specified.

1⅝ yards of black tone-on-tone fabric for blocks
24 fat quarters in various prints of pink, red,
    burgundy, brown, and beige for blocks
⅝ yard of black fabric for binding
4 yards of fabric for backing
70" x 82" piece of batting

Cutting

Cut all strips across the width of fabric.

From the black tone-on-tone fabric, cut:
24 strips, 2" x 42"; crosscut each strip into 2 strips,
    2" x 21" (48 total)

From *each* of the 24 fat quarters, cut:
2 strips, 2" x 21" (48 total)
2 strips, 3½" x 21" (48 total); crosscut each strip
    into 5 squares, 3½" x 3½" (240 total)

From the black binding fabric, cut:
7 strips, 2½" x 42"

Piecing the Blocks

1. Sew a print 2" x 21" strip to a black 2" x
   21" strip to make a strip set. Press the seam
   allowances toward the black fabric. Make a
   total of 48 strip sets. Crosscut each strip set into
   10 segments, 2" wide (480 total).

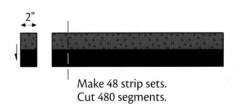

Make 48 strip sets.
Cut 480 segments.

2. Sew two matching segments together as shown
   to make a four-patch unit. Make 240 units.

Make 240.

3. Sew a matching print 3½" square to one side of each four-patch unit. Press the seam allowances toward the 3½" square. Sew two of these sections together to make one block. Press the seam allowances to one side. Make 120 blocks.

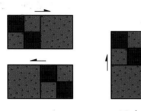

Make 120.

Assembling the Quilt Top

1. Arrange the blocks into 12 rows of 10 blocks each, rotating the blocks to form the chain as shown.
2. Sew the blocks together into rows, and then sew the rows together. Press.

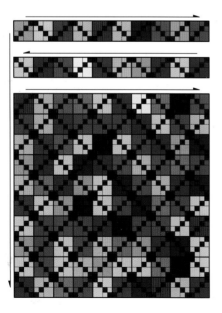

Finishing the Quilt

Refer to "Finishing Basics" on page 11 for detailed instructions as needed.

1. Layer the backing, batting, and quilt top. Baste.
2. Quilt as desired. Our quilt has an allover feather design.
3. Bind the quilt using the black 2½"-wide strips.

Inspiring Ideas

Use a quilt as a tablecloth to dress up a holiday event. Even simple snack food looks stunning when the table is set with a gorgeous quilt, some greenery, and a few candles. Serve your snacks in colored bowls that complement the shades of the quilt.

It's always a good idea to burn candles in a container meant for that purpose, and consider using unscented candles around food. To avoid food stains on your quilt, try serving candies or dry snacks that won't drip or spill.

Winter Whimsy Wool Runner

Add a bit of whimsy to your Christmas table! This simple, cheerful runner looks great on its own or as a backdrop for other seasonal decorations. Add a bowl of scented pinecones for a primitive, country look.

FINISHED SIZE: 14" x 45"

Materials

Yardages are based on 42"-wide cotton fabric and 54"-wide wool.

½ yard of cream felted wool for background
10" x 16" piece of green felted wool for trees
5" x 13" piece of brown felted wool for tree trunks
4" x 7" piece of gold felted wool for stars
8" x 10" piece of red felted wool for hearts
⅓ yard of green cotton fabric for binding
1⅜ yards of fabric for backing
1 yard of lightweight fusible web for appliqués
13 red buttons in various diameters from ¼" to ¾"
Thread for blanket-stitching around appliqué
    shapes

Cutting

Cut all strips across the width of fabric.

From the cream felted wool, cut:
1 piece, 14" x 45"

From the green cotton fabric, cut:
4 strips, 2½" x 42"

From the fabric for backing, cut:
1 piece, 14" x 45"

Appliqué

1. Referring to "Appliquéing with Wool" on page 9 and using the patterns on pages 37 and 38, prepare the following:
   - 2 each of A, B, C, and D from green felted wool
   - 2 tree trunks from brown felted wool
   - 2 stars from gold felted wool
   - 4 hearts from red felted wool
2. Arrange the shapes on the cream felted wool as shown. Appliqué the shapes by hand or machine.

Designed and made by Jeanne Large.

Finishing the Runner

This project is finished without batting or quilting. We used a preshrunk flannel as backing. Combined with the felted wool, this gives the runner a very soft, supple texture.

1. Baste the runner top to the backing.
2. Referring to "Binding" on page 12, bind the runner with the green 2½"-wide strips.
3. If you choose to do some quilting in this project, you could complement the appliqué shapes by outlining each one ¼" from the outside edge of the shape.
4. Sew the red buttons between the hearts as shown in the photo.

┌ From The Quilt Patch ┐

Sort your buttons by color into glass jars and group the jars on a shelf for a fun, eye-catching display in your sewing room.

~ Shelley

This folksy runner makes a great accent in any room. Use it on a table, a dresser, or drape it over the back of a chair. Walk around your house and audition the runner in different spots. Even a small project such as this can add a touch of Christmas merriment to a room!

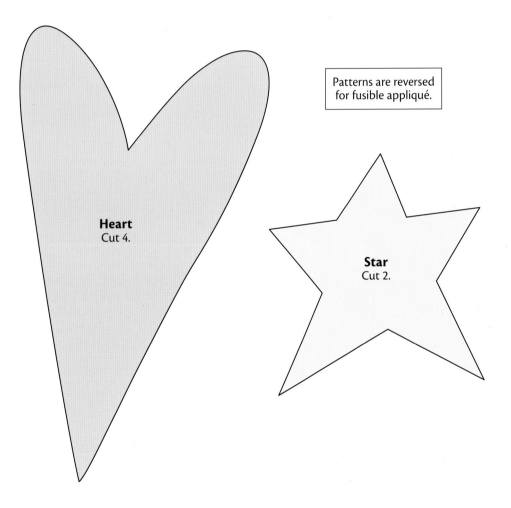

Patterns are reversed for fusible appliqué.

Heart
Cut 4.

Star
Cut 2.

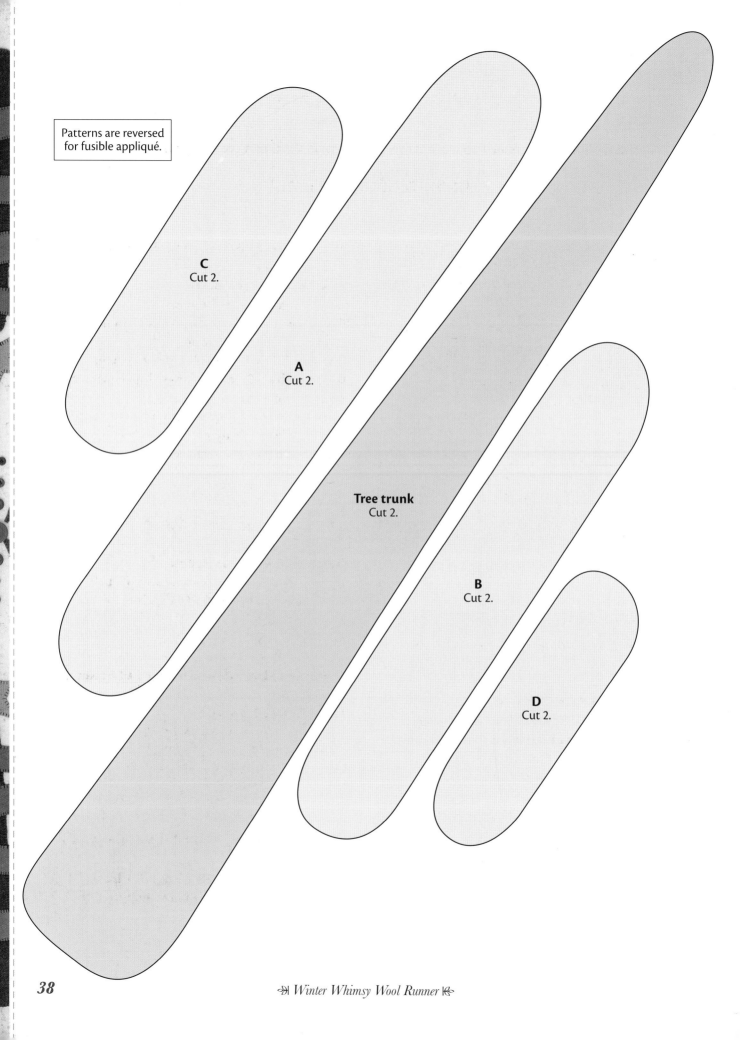

Patterns are reversed
for fusible appliqué.

C
Cut 2.

A
Cut 2.

Tree trunk
Cut 2.

B
Cut 2.

D
Cut 2.

The Stockings Were Hung

This quilt, with its chunky appliqué and minimal piecing, makes a great beginner project!

FINISHED QUILT: 58½" x 62½"

Designed and made by Jeanne Large.

Materials

Yardages are based on 40"-wide flannel and 42"-wide cotton fabric.

3 yards of black flannel for background
1⅛ yards of red fabric for sashing and binding
10" x 20" piece of dark red fabric for stocking, heel, and toe
10" x 20" piece of light red fabric for stocking, heel, and toe
10" x 20" piece of dark blue fabric for stocking, heel, and toe
10" x 20" piece of light blue fabric for stocking, heel, and toe
10" x 20" piece of dark green fabric for stocking, heel, and toe

10" x 20" piece of light green fabric for stocking, heel, and toe
⅓ yard of gold fabric for stars
½ yard of green fabric for trees
8" x 11" piece of brown fabric for tree trunks
3¾ yards of fabric for backing
3 yards of lightweight fusible web for appliqués
Thread for blanket-stitching around appliqué shapes
White graphite paper
1 skein of white embroidery cotton
67" x 71" piece of batting
18 assorted buttons, 1" diameter

Cutting

Cut all strips across the width of fabric.

From the black flannel, cut:
3 strips, 12½" x 40"; crosscut each strip into 2 rectangles, 12½" x 19½" (6 total)
4 strips, 6½" x 40"
4 strips, 8½" x 40"

From the red fabric for sashing and binding, cut:
9 strips, 2" x 42"; crosscut:
    2 strips into 4 pieces, 2" x 19½"
    4 strips into 4 pieces, 2" x 39½"
6 strips, 2½" x 42", for binding

Appliqué

1. Cut one of the 6½" x 40" black flannel strips to 6½" x 39½".
2. Sew the four 8½" x 40" black flannel strips together end to end. From this strip cut two pieces, 62½" long.

3. Referring to "Fusible-Web Appliqué" on page 7 and using the patterns on pages 43–48, prepare the following. Tape the top, middle, and bottom pattern sections of the tree together. Tape the top and bottom pattern sections of the stocking together.

- 1 stocking, 1 heel, and 1 toe from each of the 6 red, blue, and green stocking fabrics
- 11 stars from gold fabric
- 2 trees from green fabric
- 2 tree trunks from brown fabric

4. Using the photo and illustrations as a guide, arrange the shapes on the appropriate fabric pieces. Appliqué them by hand or machine.

The six 12½" x 19½" black flannel rectangles are for the stocking shapes.

The 6½" x 39½" black flannel strip is for the center strip of stars.

The two 8½" x 62½" black flannel strips are for the outer-border strips of trees and stars.

Assembling the Quilt Top

1. Arrange three of the stocking blocks and two red 2" x 19½" sashing strips into a row. Sew together. Press.

2. Repeat with the three remaining stocking blocks and two red 2" x 19½" sashing strips. Press.

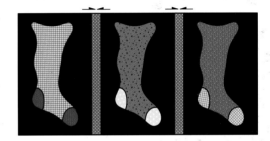

3. Sew a red 2" x 39½" sashing strip to each long edge of the center star appliqué strip. Press.

Inspiring Ideas

After the holidays, your beautiful seasonal quilts needn't be hidden away. Fold them up and stack them among other textiles on a shelf, dresser, or even the floor. This is a sure way to add a splash of color in any room and a glimmer of good cheer all year long.

4. Sew one stocking appliqué panel to the top of the star strip and one to the bottom. Press.

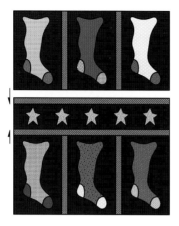

5. Sew the two remaining red 2" x 39½" sashing strips to the top and bottom of the quilt center. Press the seam allowances toward the red sashing strips.

6. Sew the three remaining red 2" x 42" sashing strips end to end to make one continuous strip. From this strip cut two strips, 50½" long. Sew the strips to the sides of the quilt center. Press the seam allowances toward the red sashing strips.

7. Sew the three 6½" x 40" black flannel strips together end to end to make one continuous strip. From this strip cut two strips, 42½" long. Sew the strips to the top and bottom of the quilt top. Press.

8. Sew the outer-border strips of trees and stars to each side of the quilt top. Press.

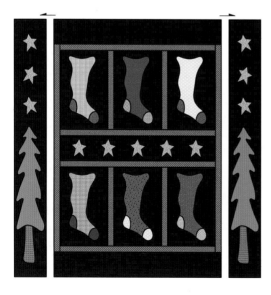

9. An easy way to transfer the words on pages 48–53 to top and bottom borders is by using white graphite paper. Lay the black border flat on a hard surface. Place the white graphite paper over the fabric. Position the words to be transferred as you want them to appear on the fabric. With a pencil, trace over the words, using enough pressure for the transfer to be effective. Stitch the words with white embroidery floss and a simple running stitch. Refer to "Hand Embroidery Stitches" on page 10.

- *From The Quilt Patch* -

Keep a lint roller in your sewing room. It comes in handy for cleaning stray threads from your ironing board, clothes, or black fabric.

~ Jeanne

Finishing the Quilt

Refer to "Finishing Basics" on page 11 for detailed instructions as needed.

1. Layer the backing, batting, and quilt top. Baste.
2. Quilt as desired. Our quilt has an allover design of stars and loops.
3. Bind the quilt using the red 2½"-wide strips.
4. Sew three buttons to the top of each stocking.

Stocking (top)
Cut 6 of complete pattern.

Pattern sections are reversed
for fusible appliqué.

Join to stocking (bottom).

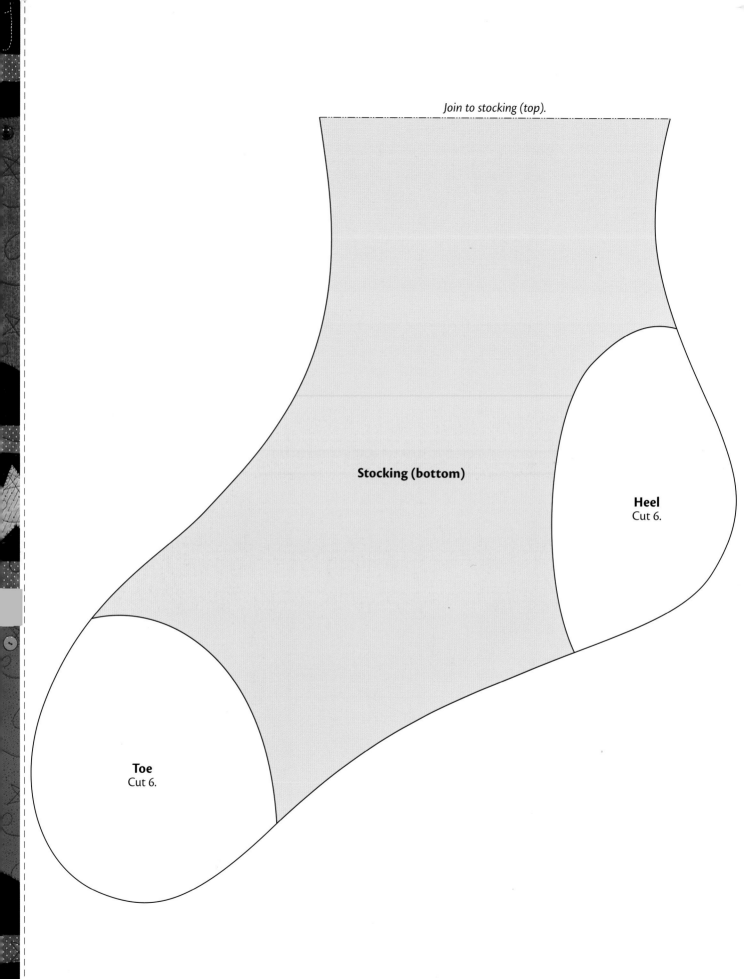

Join to stocking (top).

Stocking (bottom)

Heel
Cut 6.

Toe
Cut 6.

Tree (top)
Cut 2 of complete pattern.

Pattern sections are reversed
for fusible appliqué.

Join to tree (middle).

Join to tree (top).

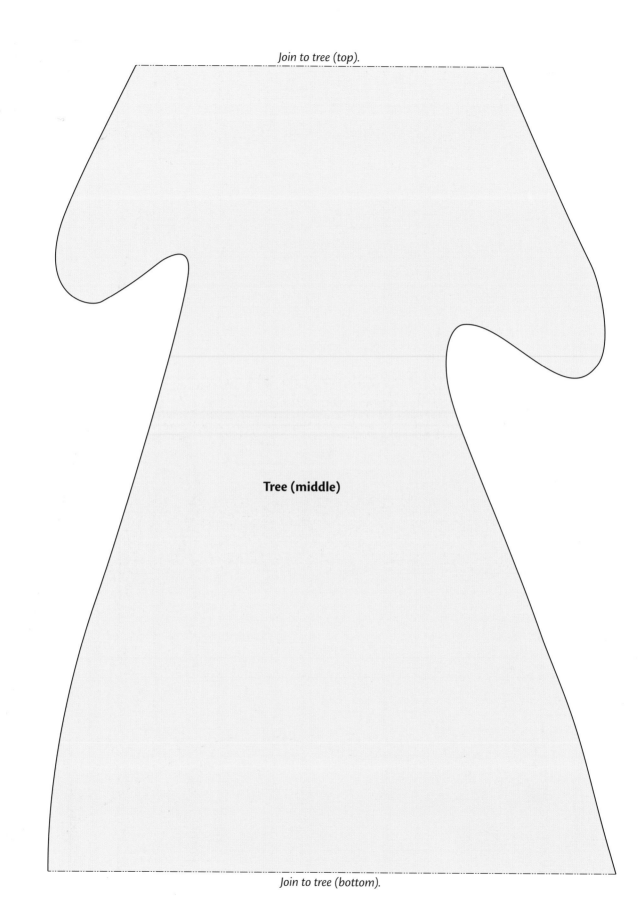

Tree (middle)

Join to tree (bottom).

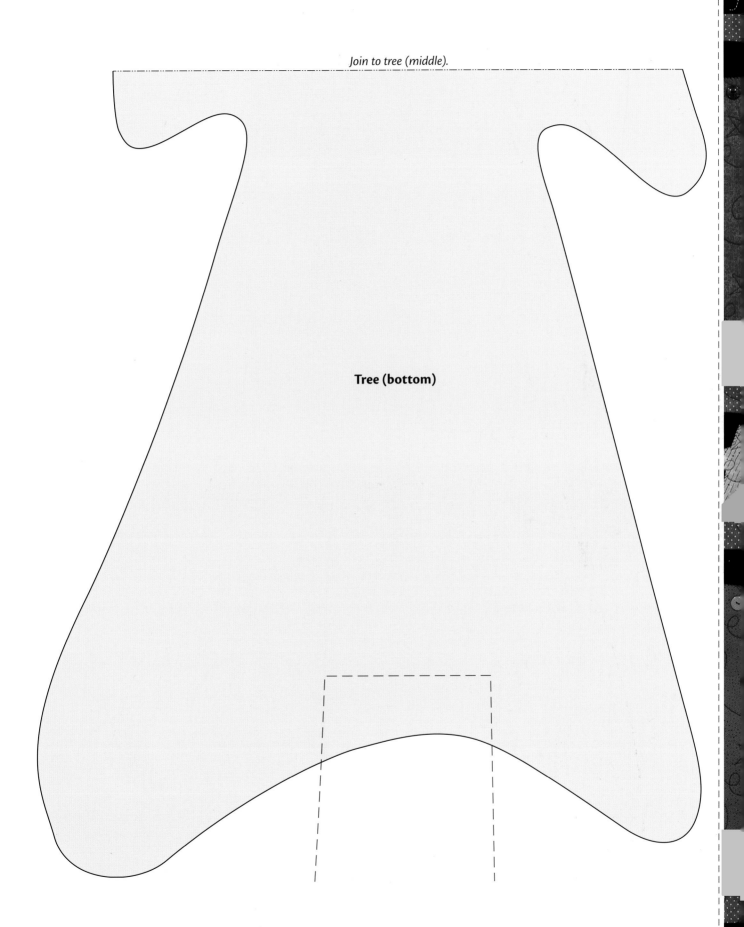

Join to tree (middle).

Tree (bottom)

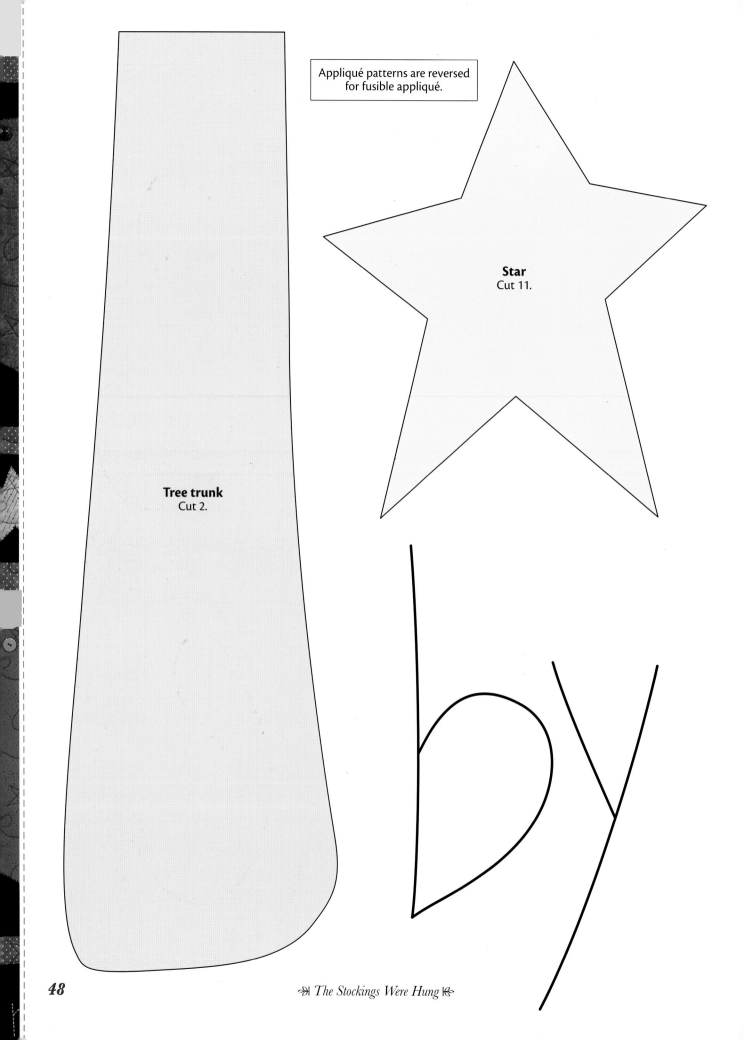

Appliqué patterns are reversed for fusible appliqué.

Star
Cut 11.

Tree trunk
Cut 2.

by

chim
ney

The Stockings Were Hung

Snowballs

This quilt offers the perfect opportunity to use lots of scraps of fabric. Pick any colorway for your snowballs, and then throw in one odd-colored snowball as a surprise!

FINISHED QUILT: 48½" x 64½"
FINISHED BLOCK: 8" x 8"

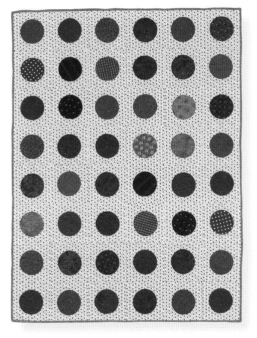

Designed and made by Shelley Wicks and Jeanne Large.
Machine quilted by Laila Nelson.

Materials

Yardages are based on 42"-wide fabric.

3⅛ yards of light cream print for background

47 squares, 6" x 6", of assorted red fabrics

1 square, 6" x 6", of contrasting fabric

½ yard of red fabric for binding

3⅛ yards of fabric for backing

56" x 72" piece of batting

2¾ yards of lightweight fusible interfacing for appliqués

Thread for blanket-stitching around appliqué shapes

Cutting

All strips are cut across the width of fabric.

From the light cream print, cut:
12 strips, 8½" x 42"; crosscut each strip into 4 squares, 8½" x 8½" (48 total)

From the red binding fabric, cut:
6 strips, 2½" x 42"

From the fusible interfacing, cut:
16 strips, 6" x 18"; crosscut each strip into 3 squares, 6" x 6" (48 total)

Making the Blocks

1. Make a template for the circle. Fold a 6" piece of paper in half, and then in half again. Trace the quarter-circle pattern on page 56 onto a separate piece of paper and cut it out. Place the quarter circle on one quarter of the folded paper and trace around the edge. Cut on the drawn line and open the paper to yield a 5" diameter circle.

2. Referring to "Fusible-Interfacing Appliqué" on page 8 and using the circle template from step 1, prepare 47 red circles and one contrasting circle.

3. Place one circle in the center of each 8½" square background block and press in place. Appliqué the shapes by hand or machine.

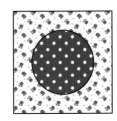

Make 48.

55

Inspiring Ideas

Use this quilt as a splash of color in a bedroom, living room, or family room. Set out a glass bowl full of red Christmas ornaments to complement the snowballs. Lots of candies are available in red and white; fill a jar or pretty dish with sweets to continue the theme. A few accents such as these placed close to the quilt will warm up the room with a rich feeling of color.

Assembling the Quilt Top

1. Arrange the blocks into eight rows of six blocks each, placing the contrasting snowball randomly in the quilt.
2. Sew the blocks together into rows. Press the seam allowances in opposite directions from row to row. Sew the rows together. Press.

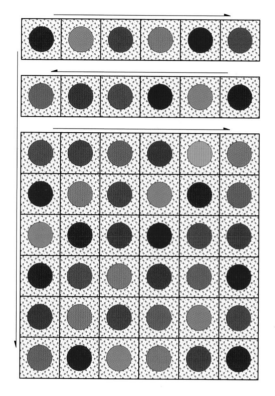

Finishing the Quilt

Refer to "Finishing Basics" on page 11 for detailed instructions as needed.

1. Layer the backing, batting, and quilt top. Baste.
2. Quilt as desired. Ours is quilted with an allover design.
3. Bind the quilt using the red 2½"-wide strips.

┌─ *From The Quilt Patch* ─────────

Take this quilt idea and run with it. You can use up a multitude of scraps by making circles in a variety of colors. The sky is the limit!

~ *Shelley*

└─────────────────────────

Quarter circle
See page 55 for instructions
for making circle template.
Cut 47 circles from red.
Cut 1 circle from contrasting color.

To All a Good Night

Spend a cozy Christmas Eve with this quilt, while visions of sugarplums and Christmas wishes dance through your head!

FINISHED QUILT: 67½" x 85½"
FINISHED BLOCK: 9" x 9"

Designed and made by Shelley Wicks and Jeanne Large.
Machine quilted by Laila Nelson.

Materials

Yardages are based on 42"-wide fabric unless otherwise specified.

2⅝ yards of green fabric for outer border
1½ yards of black fabric for blocks and letters
½ yard of brown fabric for inner border
8 fat quarters of assorted red fabrics for blocks and circle appliqués
8 fat eighths (9" x 21") of assorted green fabrics for blocks
4 fat quarters of assorted beige fabrics for blocks
2 fat quarters of assorted gold fabrics for stars
3 pieces, 8" x 10", of assorted brown fabrics for reindeer
3 pieces, 2" x 5", of assorted blue fabrics for bell harness on reindeer
4" x 10" piece of black fabric for reindeer hooves
2" x 3" piece of red fabric for reindeer noses
2" x 3" piece of white fabric for reindeer eyes
¾ yard of black fabric for binding
5¼ yards of fabric for backing
75" x 93" piece of batting
2 yards of lightweight fusible web for appliqués
Thread for blanket-stitching around appliqué shapes
15 bells, ¼" diameter
Black embroidery floss
Black fabric marker

The materials list contains sufficient fabric to make the quilt. The actual quilt is more scrappy than what's called for. If you enjoy a more scrappy look, feel free to add more fabrics.

Cutting

Cut all strips across the width of fabric unless otherwise specified.

From *each* of the 8 red fat quarters, cut:
4 strips, 3½" x 21" (32 total); crosscut each strip into 5 squares, 3½" x 3½" (160 total; 7 will be extra)

From *each* of the 8 green fat eighths, cut:
2 strips, 3½" x 21" (16 total); crosscut each strip into 5 squares, 3½" x 3½" (80 total; 8 will be extra)

From *each* of the 4 beige fat quarters, cut:
8 strips, 1½" x 21" (32 total; 1 will be extra)

From the black fabric for blocks, cut:
19 strips, 1½" x 42"; crosscut into 38 strips, 1½" x 21"

From the brown inner-border fabric, cut:
6 strips, 2½" x 42"

From the green outer-border fabric, cut:
8 strips, 9½" x 42"

From the black binding fabric, cut:
8 strips, 2½" x 42"

Piecing the Double Nine Patch Blocks

1. Sew a black 1½" x 21" strip to each long side of a beige 1½" x 21" strip to make strip set A. Press the seam allowances toward the black strips. Make a total of 15 A strip sets. Cut each strip set into 12 segments, 1½" wide (180 total).

Strip set A.
Make 15. Cut 180 segments.

2. Sew matching beige 1½" x 21" strips to the long edges of a black 1½" x 21" strip to make strip set B. Press the seam allowances toward the black strip. Make a total of 8 B strip sets. Cut each strip set into 12 segments, 1½" wide (96 total; 6 will be extra).

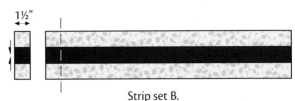

Strip set B.
Make 8. Cut 90 segments.

3. Sew two A segments and one B segment with matching beige fabric together to make a nine-patch unit. Press the seam allowances away from the center segment. Make 90 units.

Make 90.

4. Arrange five nine-patch units and four green 3½" squares to form a block. Sew them together into three rows, pressing the seam allowances toward the green squares. Sew the rows together and press the seam allowances toward the center row. Make 18 green Double Nine Patch blocks.

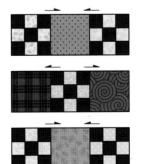
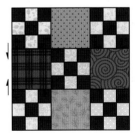

Make 18.

Make a guest room fun and inviting by using this delightful quilt on the bed. Add red and green pillows and a stuffed reindeer. Lay some garland along the headboard, strung with miniature white lights and stars for additional sparkle. Voilà, another room ready for the holidays!

Piecing the Nine Patch Blocks

Arrange nine 3½" assorted red squares into three rows of three squares each. Sew the squares together to make three rows. Press the seam allowances as shown. Sew the rows together. Press the seam allowances away from the center row. Make 17 red Nine Patch blocks.

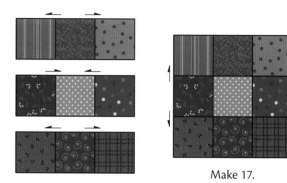

Make 17.

Assembling the Quilt Top

1. Arrange the 18 green Double Nine Patch blocks and the 17 red Nine Patch blocks into rows, alternating the color placement as shown.
2. Sew the blocks together into rows. Press the seam allowances toward the red blocks. Sew the rows together. Press the seam allowances in one direction.

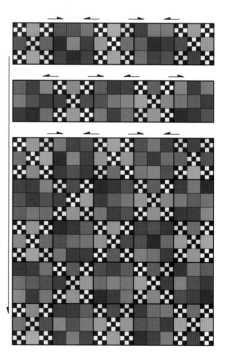

Adding the Borders

1. Sew the brown 2½" x 42" inner-border strips together end to end to make one continuous strip. From this strip, cut two strips, 63½" long, and two strips, 49½" long. Sew the 63½"-long strips to the sides of the quilt. Press. Sew the 49½"-long strips to the top and bottom of the quilt. Press.
2. Sew the green 9½" x 42" outer-border strips together end to end to make one continuous strip. From this strip, cut four strips, 67½" long. Sew two strips to the sides of the quilt. Press. Sew two strips to the top and bottom of the quilt. Press.

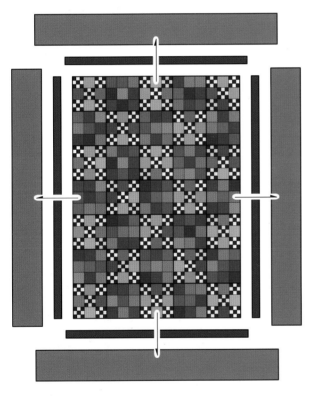

Appliquéing the Borders

1. Referring to "Fusible-Web Appliqué" on page 7 and using the patterns on pages 62–67, cut the following:
   - Letters to spell "Merry Christmas to all, and to all a good night!" from black fabric
   - 5 large stars and 5 small stars from gold fabric
   - 3 reindeer (consisting of head, body, tail, and legs) from brown fabric
   - 3 bell harnesses from blue fabric
   - 12 reindeer hooves from black fabric
   - 3 reindeer noses and 12 circles from red fabric
   - 6 reindeer eyes from white fabric
2. Referring to the photo on page 57 as a guide, arrange the shapes on the borders as shown. Press in place. Appliqué them by hand or machine.

Embroidering the Reindeer

Trace the antlers and mouth onto the reindeer. Referring to "Hand Embroidery Stitches" on page 10, stitch these details using a simple backstitch.

Finishing the Quilt

Refer to "Finishing Basics" on page 11 as needed for detailed instructions.
1. Layer the backing, batting, and quilt top. Baste.
2. Quilt as desired. Ours is quilted with an allover design.
3. Bind the quilt using the black 2½"-wide strips.
4. Hand sew five bells to each bell harness. Dot the eyes with a black fabric marker.

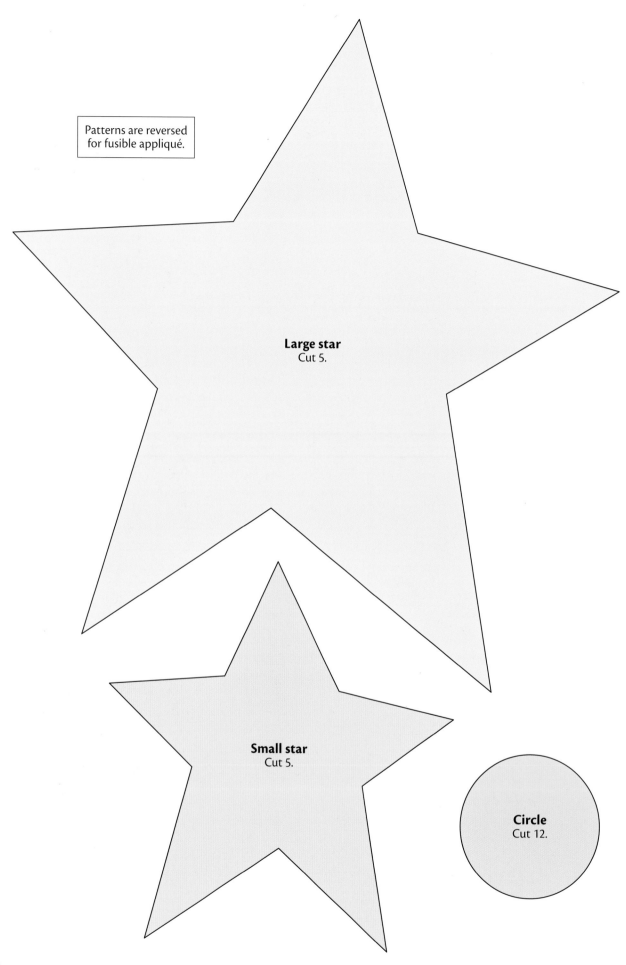

Patterns are reversed
for fusible appliqué.

Large star
Cut 5.

Small star
Cut 5.

Circle
Cut 12.

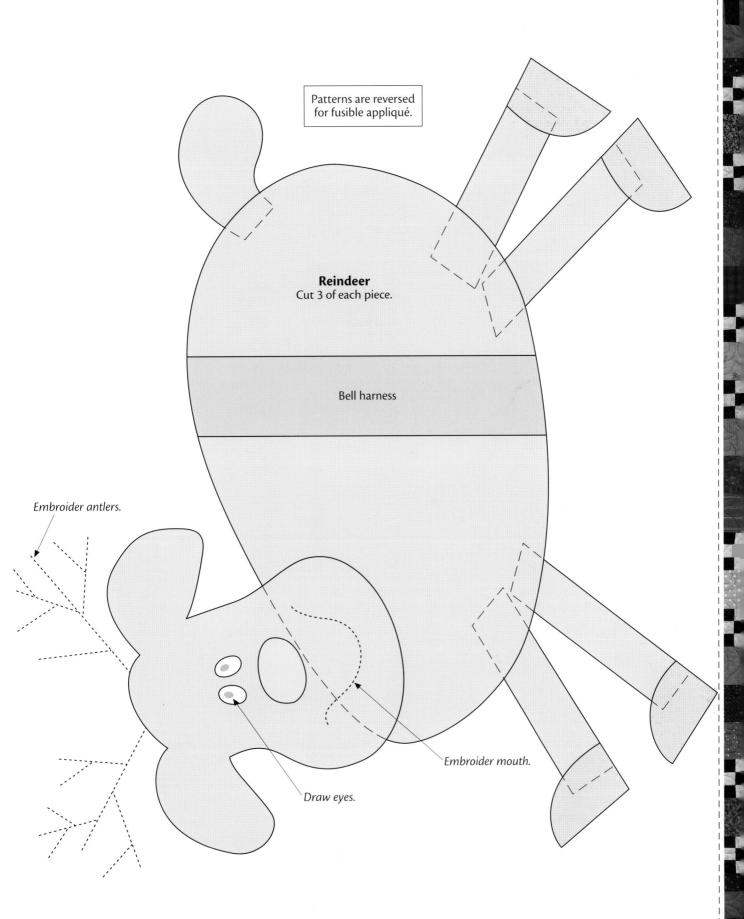

Patterns are reversed
for fusible appliqué.

Reindeer
Cut 3 of each piece.

Bell harness

Embroider antlers.

Embroider mouth.

Draw eyes.

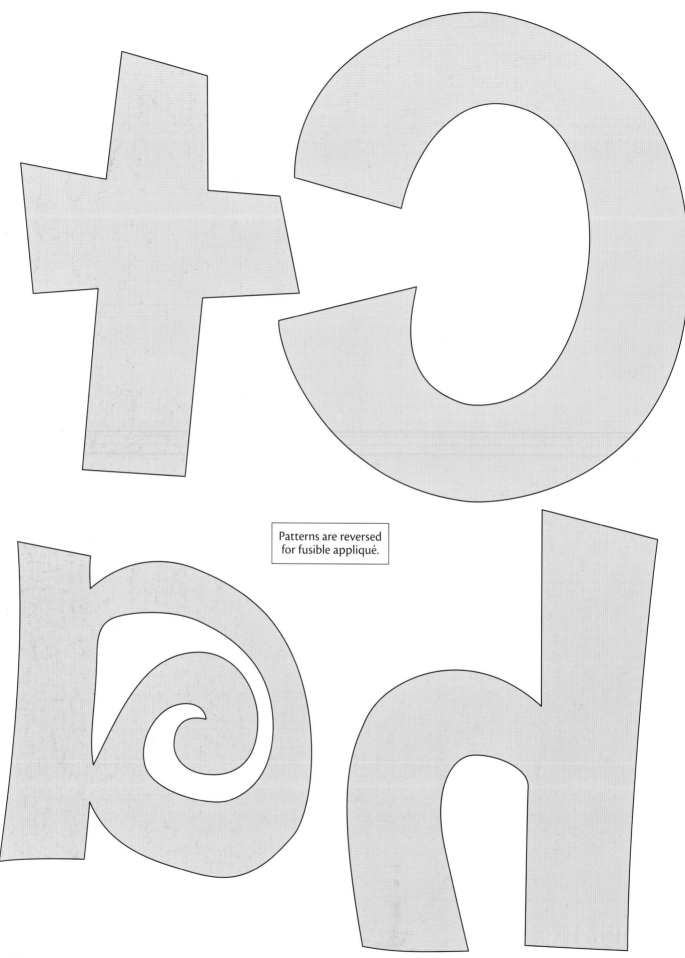

Patterns are reversed
for fusible appliqué.

Patterns are reversed
for fusible appliqué.

Patterns are reversed
for fusible appliqué.

To All a Good Night

Patterns are reversed
for fusible appliqué.

Holiday Stars Trio

Stars are a great accent at any time of the year, but truly lend themselves to holiday decorations. This trio of projects will add a touch of sparkle and charm to any room.

Holiday Stars Lap Quilt

FINISHED QUILT: 46½" x 62½"
FINISHED BLOCK: 8" x 8"

*Designed and made by Shelley Wicks and Jeanne Large.
Machine quilted by Shelley Wicks.*

Materials

Yardages are based on 42"-wide fabric.

9 fat quarters of assorted red fabrics for blocks and
 outer border
9 fat quarters of assorted green fabrics for blocks
 and outer border
⅓ yard of gold fabric for inner border
⅓ yard of gold fabric for star appliqués
½ yard of green fabric for binding
3 yards of fabric for backing
55" x 71" piece of batting

1 yard of lightweight fusible web for appliqués
Thread for blanket-stitching around appliqué shapes

*The materials list contains sufficient fabric to make the quilt.
The actual quilt is more scrappy than what's called for. If
you enjoy a more scrappy look, feel free to add more fabrics.*

Cutting

*Cut all strips across the width of fabric unless otherwise
specified.*

From *each* of the 9 red fat quarters, cut:
1 strip, 4½" x 21"; crosscut each strip into 2
 squares, 4½" x 4½" (18 total)
1 strip, 2½" x 21"; crosscut each strip into 4
 rectangles, 2½" x 4½" (36 total; 2 will be extra)
2 strips, 2½" x 21"; crosscut each strip into 2
 rectangles, 2½" x 8½" (36 total; 2 will be extra)
1 strip, 2½" x 21" (9 total)

From *each* of the 9 green fat quarters, cut:
1 strip, 4½" x 21"; crosscut each strip into 2
 squares, 4½" x 4½" (18 total; 1 will be extra)
1 strip, 2½" x 21"; crosscut each strip into 4
 rectangles, 2½" x 4½" (36 total)
2 strips, 2½" x 21"; crosscut each strip into 2
 rectangles, 2½" x 8½" (36 total)
1 strip, 2½" x 21" (9 total)

From the gold inner-border fabric, cut:
5 strips, 1½" x 42"

From the green binding fabric, cut:
6 strips, 2½" x 42"

Piecing the Blocks

1. Sew matching red 2½" x 4½" rectangles to
    opposite sides of a green 4½" square. Press
    seam allowances toward the red. Make 17 units.

Make 17.

2. Sew matching red 2½" x 8½" rectangles to the
    top and bottom of a unit made in step 1. Press

Inspiring Ideas

The size and simplicity of this quilt make it easy to visualize in other colorways. Pick any two colors that complement each other, or use light and dark shades of one color. The sky is the limit! Make one, make several—a quilt is a wonderful gift any time of the year.

the seam allowances toward the red. Make 17 blocks with green centers.

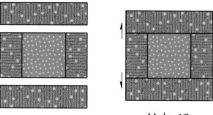

Make 17.

3. Following steps 1 and 2, reverse the color placement to make 18 blocks with red centers.

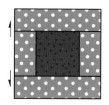

Make 18.

Assembling the Quilt Top

1. Arrange the blocks into seven rows of five blocks each. Starting with a green block in the top right corner, alternate the red and green blocks. When you're satisfied with your arrangement, make sure that each block is also positioned so that the green blocks have the long strips on the top and bottom and the red blocks have the long strips on the sides. This makes for easier stitching!

2. Sew the blocks together into rows, and then sew the rows together. Press.

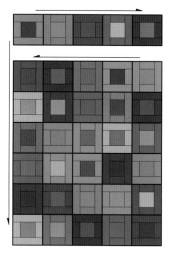

Adding the Borders

1. Sew the gold $1\frac{1}{2}$" x 42" inner-border strips together end to end to make one continuous strip. From this strip, cut two strips, $56\frac{1}{2}$" long, and two strips, $42\frac{1}{2}$" long. Sew the $56\frac{1}{2}$"-long strips to the sides of the quilt. Press. Sew the $42\frac{1}{2}$"-long strips to the top and bottom of the quilt. Press.

2. To make the scrappy outer border, use the remaining $2\frac{1}{2}$"-wide strips of red and green. Cut the strips into random lengths and sew them together end to end to make one continuous strip approximately 220" long. Press the seam allowances in one direction.

3. From this strip, cut two strips, $58\frac{1}{2}$" long, and two strips, $46\frac{1}{2}$" long. Sew the $58\frac{1}{2}$"-long strips to the sides of the quilt. Press. Sew the $46\frac{1}{2}$"-long strips to the top and bottom of the quilt. Press.

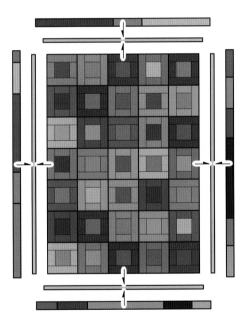

Appliquéing the Stars

1. Referring to "Fusible-Web Appliqué" on page 7 and using the star patterns at right, prepare the following from gold fabric:
   - 17 large stars
   - 18 small stars

2. Using the photo on page 69 as a guide, randomly place one star on each block. Press in place. Appliqué them by hand or machine.

Finishing the Quilt

Refer to "Finishing Basics" on page 11 for detailed instructions as needed.

1. Layer the backing, batting, and quilt top. Baste.
2. Quilt as desired. Ours is machine quilted with an allover design.
3. Bind the quilt using the green $2\frac{1}{2}$"-wide strips.

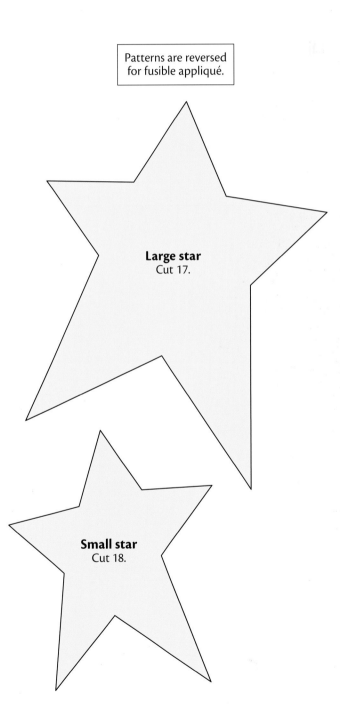

Patterns are reversed for fusible appliqué.

Large star
Cut 17.

Small star
Cut 18.

Holiday Stars Runner

FINISHED SIZE: 22½" x 50½"
FINISHED BLOCK: 4" x 4"

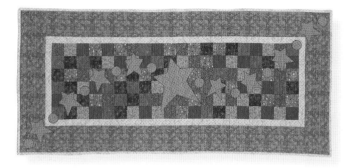

Designed and made by Jeanne Large.

Materials

Yardages are based on 42"-wide fabric unless otherwise specified.

3 fat eighths (9" x 21") of assorted red fabrics
    for blocks
3 fat eighths (9" x 21") of assorted green fabrics
    for blocks
⅝ yard of light green fabric for inner border
    and binding
¾ yard of dark green fabric for outer border
⅓ yard of gold fabric for stars and circles
1⅝ yards of fabric for backing
28" x 56" piece of batting
1 yard of lightweight fusible web for appliqués
Thread for blanket-stitching around appliqué
    shapes

Cutting

Cut all strips across the width of fabric unless otherwise specified.

From *each* of the 3 red fat eighths, cut:
3 strips, 2½" x 21" (9 total)

From *each* of the 3 green fat eighths, cut:
3 strips, 2½" x 21" (9 total)

From the light green inner-border and binding fabric, cut:
4 strips, 2½" x 42"
3 strips, 1½" x 42"

- crosscut 1 strip into 2 pieces, 1½" x 14½"
- trim 2 strips to 1½" x 40½"

From the dark green outer-border fabric, cut:
5 strips, 4½" x 42"

Piecing the Blocks

1. Sew a red 2½" x 21" strip and a green 2½" x 21" strip together to make a strip set. Press seam allowances toward the red. Make nine strip sets. Cut the strip sets into a total of 60 segments, 2½" wide.

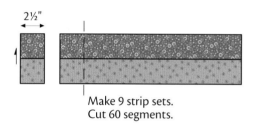

Make 9 strip sets.
Cut 60 segments.

2. Sew together two red-and-green segments to make a four-patch unit. Make 30 four-patch units.

Make 30.

3. Arrange the four-patch units into three rows of 10 units each. Sew the units together into rows. Press the seam allowances in opposite directions from row to row. Sew the rows together. Press.

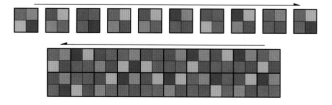

Adding the Borders

1. Sew a light green 1½" x 40½" inner-border strip to each long side of the runner. Press.
2. Sew a light green 1½" x 14½" inner-border strip to each short end of the runner. Press.
3. Sew the dark green 4½"-wide outer-border strips together end to end to make one continuous strip. From this strip, cut two strips, 42½" long, and two strips, 22½" long. Sew the 42½"-long strips to the long sides of the runner. Press. Sew the 22½"-long strips to the short ends of the runner. Press.

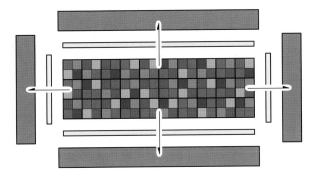

Appliquéing the Stars and Circles

1. Referring to "Fusible-Web Appliqué" on page 7 and using the circle and star patterns on page 74, prepare the following from gold fabric:
   - 1 large star
   - 8 small stars
   - 10 circles
2. Using the photo on the facing page as a guide, arrange the stars and circles on the runner. Press in place. Appliqué them by hand or machine.

Finishing the Runner

Refer to "Finishing Basics" on page 11 for detailed instructions as needed.

1. Layer the backing, batting, and runner top. Baste.
2. Quilt as desired. Ours is machine quilted with an allover design.
3. Bind the runner using the light green 2½"-wide strips.

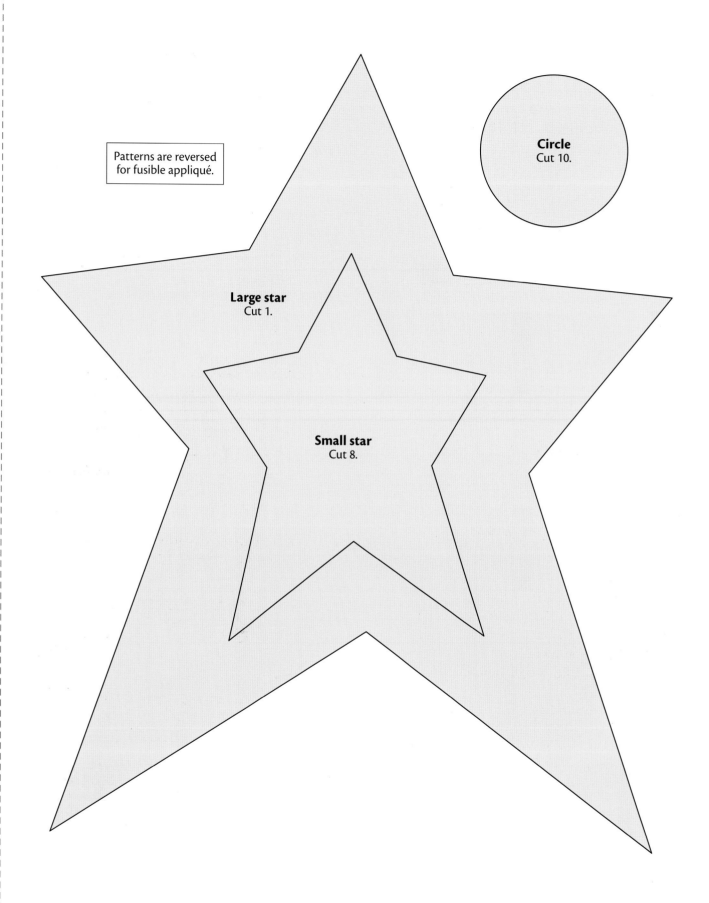

Circle
Cut 10.

Patterns are reversed for fusible appliqué.

Large star
Cut 1.

Small star
Cut 8.

Holiday Stars Pillow

FINISHED SIZE: 18" X 24"

Designed and made by Jeanne Large.

Materials

Yardages are based on 42"-wide fabric.

¼ yard *each* of 6 different red fabrics for pillow
   front and back
¼ yard of green print for pillow top
7" x 10" piece of gold fabric for stars
22" x 28" piece of batting
22" x 28" piece of muslin
7" x 10" piece of lightweight fusible web for
   appliqués
¾ yard of jumbo rickrack
11 red buttons, ¾" in diameter
Thread for blanket-stitching around appliqué shapes
Fiberfill stuffing

Cutting

*Cut all strips across the width of fabric unless otherwise
specified.*

From *each* of the 6 red fabrics, cut:
2 strips, 2½" x 42" (12 total)

From the green print, cut:
1 strip, 6½" x 42"; crosscut 1 rectangle, 6½" x 24½"

Assembling the Pillow

1. Sew the 12 red strips together along the long
   edges. Press the seam allowances in the same
   direction.

- - *From The Quilt Patch* - - - - - - - - -

*When making strip sets, we find it helpful to use
a walking foot to keep the sets from stretching and
becoming distorted. We also like to alternate the
stitching direction on each strip. This alleviates
the curving rainbow effect that comes from sewing
multiple strips together.*

~ *Shelley*

2. From the strip set, cut one segment, 12½" x
   24½", and one segment, 18½" x 24½".

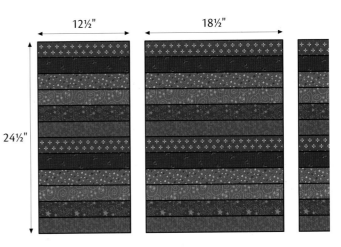

3. Sew the green 6½" x 24½" rectangle to the long edge of the red 12½" x 24½" segment. Press the seam allowances toward the green.

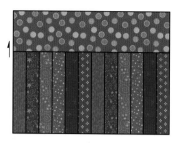

4. With right side up, lay the pillow front on top of the batting, and then the piece of muslin. Baste and quilt as desired.

5. Lay the rickrack on the seam line between the green and red segments. Stitch along both edges of the rickrack.

6. Referring to "Fusible-Web Appliqué" on page 7 and using the star pattern at right, prepare four stars from gold fabric.

7. Arrange the stars on the red segment of the pillow as shown and press in place. Appliqué by hand or machine. Sew the red buttons onto the rickrack.

8. Lay the red 18½" x 24½" strip-set segment on top of the pillow front with right sides together. Sew all around the outside edges, leaving a 6" opening along one side. Turn the pillow right side out. Stuff firmly and hand stitch the opening closed.

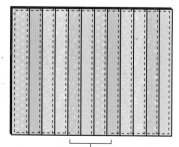

Leave a 6" opening for turning.

Inspiring Ideas

Add some cozy Christmas charm in an unexpected location by bringing your quilts into the kitchen. Lay a runner on an island or table. Drape a quilt over a chair and add a pillow. Your guests will feel your kitchen is truly the heart of your home.

Star
Cut 4.

Pattern is reversed for fusible appliqué.

❧ *Holiday Stars Pillow* ❧

Holly Sox Pillow

Feed your soul this holiday season by whipping up something just for fun.

FINISHED SIZE: 16" x 36"

Materials

Yardages are based on 42"-wide fabric.

1⅛ yards of black flannel for pillow front and back

10" x 10" piece of red striped fabric for stocking, heel, and toe

10" x 10" piece of red print for stocking, heel, and toe

10" x 10" piece of orange-and-yellow plaid for stocking, heel, and toe

10" x 10" piece of yellow print for stocking, heel, and toe

10" x 10" piece of green fabric for holly leaves

8" x 10" piece of gold fabric for stars

1⅛ yards of green jumbo rickrack

10 red buttons in various diameters from ¼" to ¾" for holly berries

1 yard of lightweight fusible web for appliqués

Thread for blanket-stitching around appliqué shapes

Fiberfill stuffing

Cutting

From the *lengthwise grain* of the black flannel, cut:

2 rectangles, 16½" x 36½"

Assembling the Pillow

1. Referring to "Fusible-Web Appliqué" on page 7 and using the patterns on the facing page, prepare the following:
   - 1 stocking, 1 heel, and 1 toe from red striped fabric
   - 1 stocking, 1 heel, and 1 toe from red print
   - 1 stocking, 1 heel, and 1 toe from orange-and-yellow plaid
   - 1 stocking, 1 heel, and 1 toe from yellow print
   - 9 holly leaves from green fabric
   - 6 stars from gold fabric

2. Using the photo on page 77 as a guide, arrange the rickrack on the pillow front and sew along both edges of the rickrack by hand or machine. Arrange the appliqué shapes and press in place. Appliqué them by hand or machine.

3. Sew the red buttons onto the rickrack in clusters for holly berries.

Designed and made by Jeanne Large.

4. Lay the pillow front and back with right sides together and raw edges even. Sew around the outside edge of the pillow, leaving a 6" opening along one edge.

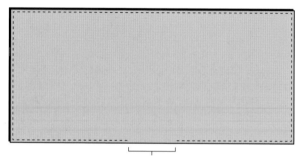

Leave a 6" opening for turning.

5. Turn the pillow right side out. Stuff firmly and hand stitch the opening closed.

Inspiring Ideas ———

A pillow makes a great hostess gift. A handmade present is truly fun to give, and always a delightful surprise to receive.

⚜ From The Quilt Patch

When removing the paper backing from appliqué shapes prepared with fusible web, fold an edge in about ¼" and the paper will separate from the shape, enabling you to easily peel it off.

~ Shelley

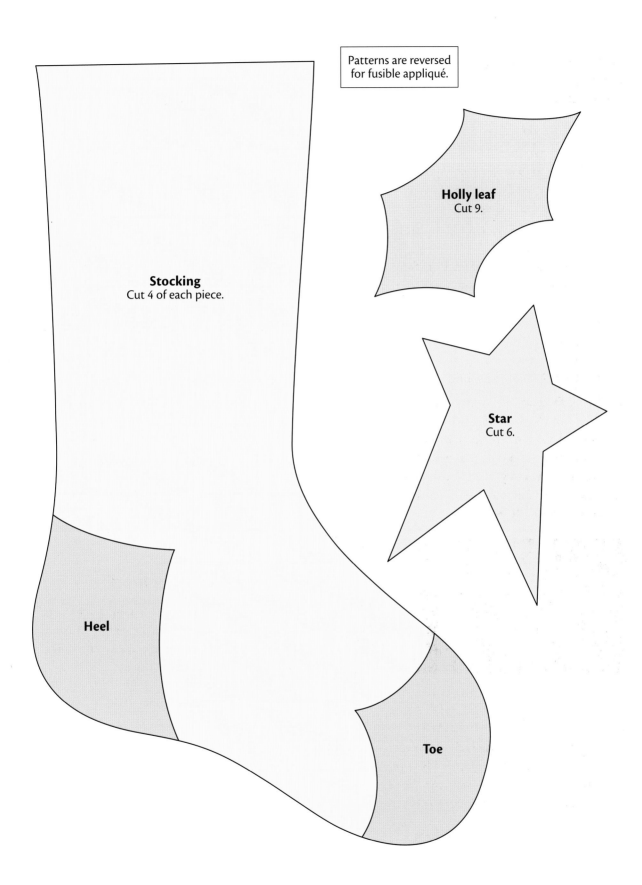

Patterns are reversed for fusible appliqué.

Holly leaf
Cut 9.

Stocking
Cut 4 of each piece.

Star
Cut 6.

Heel

Toe

About the Authors

Shelley and Jeanne

Shelley Wicks

Shelley has been quilting for well over 20 years, having started when "quilting wasn't cool"! Both her grandmothers quilted in different styles and each passed on her knowledge and love of quilting.

Shelley lives in beautiful, historic Moose Jaw, Saskatchewan, with her husband, two of her children, and one cranky cat that allows them all to continue living in the house with him! Her eldest child lives just 40 miles away, which is perfect for quick trips to visit with her grandson.

When Shelley is not busy designing, quilting, working at the shop, or away at a trade show, she enjoys shopping, home decorating, reading, and if there's still time left over, working in her yard!

Jeanne Large

Jeanne learned to sew as a young girl from her mom and her Auntie Alice. She grew up sewing garments for herself, and then moved on to sewing for her five children, often creating something original and unique. Quilting was a natural progression from garment sewing and continues to fill a need to "create." Time to spend on other hobbies such as basket weaving and woodworking is rare as the number of grandchildren grows and work commitments increase; however, there is always time to sew.

Jeanne and her husband live in a wonderful old house in Moose Jaw, Saskatchewan.

There's More Online!

Learn more about Shelley, Jeanne, and the Quilt Patch at the shop's website, www.thequiltpatch.ca. Find more great books on quilting, knitting, crochet, and more at www.martingale-pub.com

Acknowledgments

Many thanks to our families and friends, who are a constant source of love and support. This group includes our fabulous staff at the Quilt Patch, who all put in extra hours keeping the store running smoothly so we could work on "The Book."